LIFT EVERY
VOICE
AND
SING

A Celebration of the
African American National Anthem

James Weldon Johnson • illustrated by Elizabeth Catlett
foreword by Ashley Bryan

BLOOMSBURY
CHILDREN'S BOOKS
NEW YORK   LONDON   OXFORD   NEW DELHI   SYDNEY

In 1899, James Weldon Johnson was a principal at Stanton Elementary School in Jacksonville, Florida. The school, in keeping with the time period, was segregated; only black students attended. The school was planning for an upcoming celebration of Abraham Lincoln's birthday, and James Weldon Johnson wrote a poem in commemoration. He then gave the poem to his brother, composer John Rosamond Johnson, who set the poetry to music. The resulting song, "Lift Ev'ry Voice and Sing," was publicly performed for the first time on February 12, 1900, by five hundred children. The Johnson brothers' song spread in popularity, first throughout the South and then to the whole country. The National Association for the Advancement of Colored People eventually adopted it as the official African American national anthem. Today, the song is often heard in schools and churches, at celebrations and protests across the country.

FOREWORD

Elizabeth Catlett's art and the Johnson brothers' poem and hymn "Lift Every Voice and Sing" have long been sources of inspiration in my life. Elizabeth Catlett's linocuts dramatize the song. Her cutting with a linocut carving tool reminds me of a farmer stroking the earth to create a garden of vegetables or flowers. One loving stroke of her tool brings form out of the level linoleum surface, which reveals a head, a hand, a body. The book is not just a tribute to linocut but a garden of illustrations, revealing in the page: plot, images, words.

Our thanks to Elizabeth for her gift of herself as an artist.
—ASHLEY BRYAN

Linocut   13 x 19 cm   1947

Lift ev'ry voice and sing

Till earth and heaven ring,

Ring with the harmonies of Liberty;

Linocut   15 x 22.5 cm   1947

Let our rejoicing rise

High as the listening skies,

Let it resound loud as the rolling sea.

COLORED ONLY

Linocut   16 x 16 cm   1946

Sing a song full of the faith that the
dark past has taught us,

Sing a song full of the hope that the
present has brought us,

Linocut   18 x 23 cm   1946

Facing the rising sun of our new day begun

Let us march on till victory is won.

Linocut   15 x 12 cm   1946

Stony the road we trod,

Bitter the chastening rod,

Felt in the days when hope unborn had died;

Linocut   23 x 15.5 cm   1947

Yet with a steady beat,

Have not our weary feet

Come to the place for which our
fathers sighed?

Linocut   15 x 21.5 cm   1946

We have come over a way that with
    tears has been watered,

We have come, treading our path
    through the blood of the slaughtered,

Linocut   15.5 x 23 cm   1946

Out from the gloomy past,

Till now we stand at last

Where the white gleam of our bright
    star is cast.

Linocut 15.5 x 23 cm 1946

God of our weary years,

God of our silent tears,

Thou who has brought us thus far
    on the way:

Linocut   10 x 13.25 cm   1947

Thou who has by Thy might

Led us into the light,

Keep us forever in the path, we pray.

Linocut   15 x 11 cm   1946

Lest our feet stray from the places,
Our God, where we met Thee,

Lest, our hearts drunk with the wine
of the world, we forget Thee;

Linocut   15.5 x 23 cm   1947

Shadowed beneath Thy hand,

May we forever stand.

True to our GOD,

True to our native land.

When Elizabeth Catlett was awarded a Julius Rosenwald Foundation grant in the 1940s, she saw the opportunity to work on a project "for the people." She decided to focus on black women and went to Mexico to begin her series of paintings, prints, and sculpture, from which these linocuts were taken.

ELIZABETH CATLETT'S ORIGINAL CAPTIONS TO THE ART

Lift Ev'ry Voice and Sing

Lyrics by
James Weldon Johnson

Music by
J. Rosamond Johnson

poco a poco rall.

taught   us;   Sing   a   song   full of the
wa - tered;   We have come, tread-ing our
met   Thee,   Lest   our   hearts, drunk with the

poco a poco rall.

allargando   *a tempo*

hope that the pres - ent has brought   us;   Fac - ing the
path thro' the blood of the slaugh -   tered, Out from the
wine of the world, we for - get   Thee; Shad-owed be -

allargando   *sffz*   *mf*
                       a tempo

ris - ing   sun   of our new day be -
gloom - y   past.   Till now we stand at _____
neath Thy hand, May we for - ev - er _____

gun,   Let us march on till vic - to - ry _____ is won.
last Where the white gleam of our bright star _____ is cast.
stand, True to our God, True to our na - tive land.

ff

BLOOMSBURY CHILDREN'S BOOKS
Bloomsbury Publishing Inc., part of Bloomsbury Publishing Plc
1385 Broadway, New York, NY 10018

BLOOMSBURY, BLOOMSBURY CHILDREN'S BOOKS, and the Diana logo are trademarks of Bloomsbury Publishing Plc

First published in the United States of America in February 1993
by Walker Books for Young Readers, an imprint of Bloomsbury Publishing, Inc.
New edition published in January 2019 by Bloomsbury Children's Books

Bloomsbury books may be purchased for business or promotional use. For information on bulk purchases please contact Macmillan Corporate and Premium Sales Department at specialmarkets@macmillan.com

ISBN 978-1-68119-955-9 (new edition) • ISBN 978-1-68119-957-3 (e-book) • ISBN 978-1-68119-956-6 (e-PDF)

The Library of Congress has cataloged the original edition as follows:
Johnson, James, Weldon, 1871–1938.
Lift every voice and sing / James Weldon Johnson; woodcuts by Elizabeth Catlett.
p. cm.
Includes music for voice and piano.
Summary: An illustrated version of the song that has come to be considered the African American national anthem.
ISBN 0-8027-8250-7
1. Songs, English—United States—Texts. [1. Afro-Americans—Songs and music. 2. Songs.]
I. Catlett, Elizabeth, 1919–2012. ill. II. Title.
PZ8.3.J6334Li 1993   782.42164'026'8—dc20   92-27333 CIP AC

Typeset in Lumberjack
Book design by John Candell
Printed in China by Leo Paper Products, Heshan, Guangdong
2 4 6 8 10 9 7 5 3 1

To find out more about our authors and books visit www.bloomsbury.com and sign up for our newsletters.